Summary and Analysis of

THANK YOU FOR YOUR SERVICE

Based on the Book by David Finkel

WORTH BOOKS
SMART SUMMARIES

All rights reserved, including without limitation the right to reproduce this book or any portion thereof in any form or by any means, whether electronic or mechanical, now known or hereinafter invented, without the express written permission of the publisher.

This Worth Books book is based on the 2013 hardcover edition of *Thank Your for Your Service* by David Finkel published by Scribe Publications.

Summary and analysis copyright © 2017 by Open Road Integrated Media, Inc.

ISBN: 978-1-5040-0848-8

Worth Books
180 Maiden Lane
Suite 8A
New York NY 10038
www.worthbooks.com

Worth Books is a division of Open Road Integrated Media, Inc.

The summary and analysis in this book are meant to complement your reading experience and bring you closer to a great work of nonfiction. This book is not intended as a substitute for the work that it summarizes and analyzes, and it is not authorized, approved, licensed, or endorsed by the work's author or publisher. Worth Books makes no representations or warranties with respect to the accuracy or completeness of the contents of this book.

Contents

Context	1
Overview	3
Summary	7
Cast of Characters	31
Direct Quotes and Analysis	35
Trivia	41
What's That Word?	45
Critical Response	49
About David Finkel	53
For Your Information	57
Bibliography	59

Context

In an attempt to dismantle and expel al-Qaeda, and force Osama bin Laden's extrication to the United States, American troops invaded Afghanistan in 2001, and the war continued for 13 years, until 2014. Then-president of Iraq, Saddam Hussein, was accused of harboring weapons of mass destruction (WMDs), and US President George W. Bush ordered Operation Iraqi Freedom in 2003. The Iraq War continued until the last troops left in 2011.

As of 2014, there are 2.7 million veterans of the Afghanistan and Iraq Wars. Mental disorders are one of three most common diagnoses amongst veterans receiving medical treatment, constituting 55% of the 1 million veterans receiving treatment. David Fin-

SUMMARY AND ANALYSIS

kel's first book, *The Good Soldiers*, followed the men of a US infantry battalion on a 15-month tour of Iraq between 2007 and 2008; *Thank You for Your Service* picks up the story of some of these men as they return home. After depicting what happens during war, Finkel believed it was just as important to shine a light on the much less visible "after-war."

While there are many books, both nonfiction and literary, detailing the experiences of soldiers and civilians during the Iraq War, such as reporter Dexter Filkin's *The Forever War* (2008), books looking at the aftermath for soldiers are still rare. Helen Benedict's *The Lonely Soldier: The Private War of Women Serving in Iraq* (2009) focuses on the unique problems experienced by female soldiers both in conflict and after discharge. Finkel's book is atypical of Iraq memoirs insofar as it is relatively apolitical, eschewing debates over whether the invasion was justified, and instead focusing on the returned soldiers' everyday lives and mental states. The only criticisms of the army or the US government are reserved for its slowness to address the PTSD and suicide epidemic amongst veterans, although those who worked hard to change the situation are given recognition in the text. Finkel removes himself from the narration and instead places the men and their families at center stage.

Overview

Thank You for Your Service examines the progress of several Iraq veterans as they return home to America, struggling with post-traumatic stress disorder (PTSD), as well as the effects that deployment had on their loved ones. Three deployments have taken a severe toll on Adam Schumann, who returns home to Fort Riley, Kansas, wracked with guilt over the death of fellow soldier James Doster. Adam's wife, Saskia, soon becomes exhausted by the burden of taking care of their two children while dealing with her husband's outbursts, nightmares, and suicidal thoughts. Meanwhile, James Doster's widow, Amanda, remains unable to move on from the horrific death of her husband, and continues to seek

SUMMARY AND ANALYSIS

answers about how and why he died. Tausolo Aieti, a young Samoan soldier who served with Adam and James, is suffering insomnia, memory problems, and violent impulses, and despite being admitted to a treatment program for traumatized soldiers, Tausolo ends up arrested for domestic battery against his wife, Theresa. Nic DeNinno, from the same company, is suicidal and haunted by dreams of dead bodies. Michael Emory, a semi-paralyzed soldier who was rescued by Adam Schumann, suffers from PTSD and has attempted suicide; his wife left him, and he no longer trusts himself to be around his daughter.

These men are the success stories—they are still alive, while their comrades have died overseas. The suicide rate in the army is spiraling out of control, despite the concerted efforts of army chief of staff Peter Chiarelli to reduce the number. There are no clear answers; suicide prevention training and mental health treatment have limited success. Former sergeant Tim Jung knows this only too well, having nearly waded into a river and ended his life; his colleague Michael Lewis is scarred by the experience of traumatized veteran Jessie Robinson dying in his arms of an overdose. Adam, Tausolo, Nic, and Michael persist in their journey of recovery with the support of advocates like Patti Walker, the wife of a severely injured soldier, who helps them get access to benefits, jobs, and treatment programs. Even four years after his return and a great deal of therapy, Adam Schumann reflects that there are no easy answers.

Summary

Prologue

Soldier Adam Schumann is being sent home to Fort Riley after his most recent 9-month deployment in Iraq because his mental health has deteriorated. Multiple traumatic missions have compounded his fear and guilt to the point where he wants to die. Yet he feels ashamed of having to tell his squad he is leaving not for an injury, but for mental health reasons. He says his goodbyes and walks to the helicopter, ridden with guilt.

Need to Know: The wars in Afghanistan and Iraq, begun in 2001 and 2003 respectively, have left 970,000 American veterans with some form of disability.

SUMMARY AND ANALYSIS

According to the Watson Institute of International & Public Affairs, "many more live with physical and emotional scars despite lack of disability status."

1

Adam has been diagnosed with PTSD, tinnitus, and mild traumatic brain injury (TBI). He suffers from anxiety, depression, nightmares, and headaches. Two years after his departure from combat, his relationship with his wife Saskia is strained; they argue regularly and worry about money. The couple has a 6-year-old daughter named Zoe, and an infant son named Jaxson. Saskia lives in fear of Adam taking his own life.

Adam had a difficult childhood. His abusive father left when he was 6 years old; he was molested as a child by an older boy; and he was raised by a poor, single mother. When he turned nine, he moved in with his grandfather, a veteran of World War II, Korea, and Vietnam, who, despite being a violent alcoholic in his younger years, was a paternal figure and a role model for Adam. He also inspired Adam's ambition to join the army.

The couple attends an appointment for Adam at the VA hospital in Topeka, Kansas. There, Saskia thinks back to Adam's return from war, which was muted compared to other soldiers' celebratory receptions, and involved Amanda Doster, the young widow of James Doster, a fellow soldier who died in combat, who was demanding that Adam tell her what happened to her husband.

"Survivor guilt" can be a powerful barrier to recovery from trauma, and Adam's shame at surviving while his friend James died was compounded by fellow soldier Christopher Golembe telling him, "'none of this shit would have happened if you were there.'" Nancy Sherman, PhD, writes that senior ranking soldiers "routinely talk about unit members as . . . family members, their own children, of sorts, who have been entrusted to them. To fall short of unconditional care is experienced as a kind of perfidy, a failure to be faithful." Adam clearly feels he failed James and Christopher as a unit commander by staying behind while his men went out and died.

Need to Know: Army suicides in 2003, the first year of the Iraq War, outstripped deaths in combat. Despite suicide awareness prevention campaigns following this spike, they did so again in 2008.

2

Amanda Doster remains stuck in her grief for her husband James, who was in Adam Schumann's unit and was killed by a bomb during deployment. Three years later, Amanda is moving to a new home with the help of her friend Sally. Her family and friends, initially sympathetic, have become impatient with her insistence on being "so relentlessly heartbroken." When the movers arrive, Amanda insists on handling all of James' belongings herself.

Amanda became close with Saskia Schumann while their husbands were in Iraq together—Adam led the unit James was in. One night, James gave up his video call slot to Adam, "who seemed in need of it," and instead went on the mission that resulted in his death. Adam kept a fragment of shrapnel from the bomb that killed James; he gave it to Amanda Doster when she confronted him at the airport.

Need to Know: Amanda's denial that James is really gone prevents her from moving on, demonstrated by her keeping some of his everyday items—his shaving cream, his used toothbrush. She is devastated, lost, confused, and misses him dearly. The fact that the army gave her conflicting information about his death didn't help. She had to find answers herself, so she requested his autopsy report and questioned the already traumatized Adam Schumann.

3

Tausolo Aieti, a 26-year-old Samoan American, is another survivor of Adam Schumann and James Doster's unit, and is graduating from a seven-week inpatient program at a Topeka hospital for soldiers. Tausolo was severely traumatized by the death of fellow solider James Harrelson, with whom he was caught in a burning Humvee after their vehicle hit a roadside bomb. Despite rescuing two other soldiers from the vehicle and suffering a concussion and a broken leg, Tausolo has been haunted by dreams of Harrelson "on fire, asking 'Why didn't you save me?'"

When he moved back to his apartment in Geary Estates, Kansas, and joined his wife Theresa, Tausolo began drinking, taking lots of pills, and mentioning suicide. His nightmares and temper flares became worse, resulting in a week "on lockdown" in the hospital. Soon after, he joined the inpatient program at Topeka. His need for help is assessed and he is admitted to the Warrior Transition Battalion (WTB), a program based at Fort Riley to help traumatized soldiers.

Need to Know: Part of the WTB program is Cognitive Processing Therapy. This is a form of Cognitive Behavioral Therapy, which involves examining, challenging, and reframing troublesome thoughts in order to move past trauma. The National Center for PTSD, part of the VA, says on its website: "You may believe you are to blame for what happened or that the world is a dangerous place. These kinds of thoughts keep you stuck in your PTSD and cause you to miss out on things you used to enjoy. CPT

SUMMARY AND ANALYSIS

teaches you a new way to handle these upsetting thoughts."

Rates of suicide are significantly higher among veterans than among the civilian population, yet the VA only started tracking the rate of veteran suicides in 2008, five years after the Iraq War began and seven years after the invasion of Afghanistan.

4

Nic DeNinno, who was in the same company as Adam Schumann, James Doster, and Tausolo Aieti, has been transferred from the Fort Riley WTB to a psychiatric hospital in Pueblo, Colorado, after his mood swings and suicidal talk became concerning. At the hospital, DeNinno writes in his journal about nightmares, hallucinations, and persistent feelings of anger; he says he sees dead Iraqis in his bathtub. He undergoes CPT as part of a group, where soldiers read from their journals and describe the circumstances of their trauma.

His pregnant wife Sascha makes the eight-hour drive to Pueblo to see if the hospital is helping. Nic gives her his journal to read, illustrating his shame at having attacked a houseful of Iraqis only to find he had the wrong house. The two see a counselor together and Nic admits he is afraid Sascha will hate him if she knows what he did in Iraq; she tells him she does not.

Need to Know: The group therapy session has the soldiers trade tales of their cavalier attitude to dead bodies, and their lack of sympathy for Iraqis—but that was when they were trained as killing machines. Now, as civilians, they are trying to make sense of all the violence and needless carnage. The images of bodies haunt them, and the guilt of being unable to save their comrades just about destroys them. What the soldiers were experiencing is called habituation. By living in world of consistent violence, their emotional responses were dulled to the horror.

5

Adam Schumann is now working at a call center to help veterans access benefits. He hates his job and yearns to find a career that takes him outside, such as working as a park ranger, but his own benefits are too meager to support his family and so he must take what he can. He resents and plays pranks on his coworker Calvin McCloy, who was in the same unit as he was. A roadside bomb burned 40% of McCloy's body and left him with brain damage and partial deafness. Unlike Schumann, who struggles with getting to work on time and is depressed and angry, McCloy has made peace with his situation and has chosen to live the best life he can despite his physical and emotional hardships.

SUMMARY AND ANALYSIS

The army has just released a report on suicide prevention and chief of staff Peter Chiarelli answers questions about it at a press conference in Washington DC. A former commander himself, General Chiarelli now holds a monthly meeting that examines every army suicide that occurs and the events leading up to it. He and his team are trying to understand why the suicide rate is higher in soldiers than the general populace, and what the military can do to protect and support soldiers coming home from war. Unfortunately, there is still so little they understand—is it PTSD, brain damage, or personality type that increases one's risk?—but Chiarelli is working tirelessly on putting operations in place to recognize the warning signs and help soldiers in need.

Need to Know: Veteran poverty is a persistent problem in the USA. In 2006, it was estimated that 196,000 veterans were homeless, and this was set to surge after the Iraq and Afghanistan Wars. Quality employment is especially difficult for veterans suffering from emotional or physical disabilities to secure.

Peter Chiarelli's research identifies that soldiers were suffering mental breakdowns but feared stigma if they sought help—not an unjustified fear. Veterans suffering from mental and emotional trauma admit to feeling weak, confused, and humiliated.

6

Adam has bonded with a fellow veteran from his first deployment. Stephen, whom he met in the WTB, has a TBI and PTSD, and has been declared totally disabled. Despite the anguish of his wife, Christina, "for the loss of my husband. For the man he was," Saskia Schumann admits she is jealous of Stephen and his wife because they received a surprise $11,000 from the government—in contrast, the Schumanns are struggling financially.

Adam receives an email from Michael Emory, who hopes to reconnect with him. Adam rescued Michael after he was shot in the head, but he has partial paralysis and struggles with anger and violent impulses. His wife divorced him after he assaulted and threatened to kill her, and he has attempted suicide several times. Now in therapy, Michael wants to thank Adam for saving him. The two men talk about the war and go fishing together.

Eleven days later, Adam and Saskia have a fight that culminates in Adam putting a loaded shotgun to his head and telling Saskia to pull the trigger. He refuses to put the gun down until Jaxson's cries shake him from his trance. Eventually, things improve. Adam and Saskia buy a puppy for their daughter, Zoe. After the puppy breaks a leg, Adam sells his two guns to pay for the hefty veterinary bill.

SUMMARY AND ANALYSIS

Meanwhile, four more suicides at Fort Hood, Texas, are reported to Peter Chiarelli. The general in command tells Chiarelli he is reviewing all 46,500 of his soldiers to identify high-risk individuals.

Need to Know: Michael advises Adam not to give up on his struggling marriage to Saskia, and says how he regrets losing his wife, Maria, every day. Veterans have a higher rate of divorce than the rest of the US population, and single or divorced veterans have a higher rate of suicide.

Saskia admits that she swings between sympathy for Adam and believing that he is malingering unnecessarily. She finds it hard to see the point of inpatient programs if they are just going to leave the family financially disadvantaged; even with disability pay and Adam working at the call center, he is still only bringing in two-thirds of his army salary.

7

After moving, Amanda Doster has begun journaling her grief and admits that, "after nearly 3 years, I haven't hit rock bottom yet." She continues to struggle on any day remotely connected to James—his birthday, their wedding anniversary, Father's Day, and most of all, the anniversary of his death. Attending a Ceremony of Remembrance for the Fallen at Fort

Riley only makes her feel angry at the insensitivity of the army, as the families are required to stand in a receiving line shaking the hands of strangers while listening to upbeat, patriotic music. To her, it feels more like a wedding or a birthday party than a funeral.

Amanda reflects on the people to whom James's death brought her closer. She bonded with the Schumanns until they borrowed several thousand dollars, failed to repay it, and fell out of touch with her. She was good friends with Alex Boland, the lieutenant in charge of James's platoon, until he was redeployed. Now she is close with Matthew Stern, a medic who attempted to save James after he was hit, and Sally, a local friend who has been with the family for both previous anniversaries of James's death.

Amanda takes her daughters to the cemetery to visit James's headstone. The visit is difficult for Amanda, but important.

Need to Know: Like Adam Schumann and Tausolo Aieti, Matthew Stern suffered intense guilt, both for surviving when others died and also, as the unit's medic, for not being able to save his fellow solider.

Amanda Doster castigates the army for treating the Ceremony of Remembrance for the Fallen as an instance of celebration. Being thanked for her dead husband's service does little to assuage the pain of Amanda's loss; in this case it seems only to exacerbate

SUMMARY AND ANALYSIS

the isolation she feels from the army and other military families.

8

Patti Walker, an advocate for traumatized soldiers who works for the Army Wounded Warrior Program (AW2), understands the effects of PTSD and TBI only too well. She personally works with forty-nine wounded veterans, and counts her husband, Kevin, as the fiftieth. In Iraq, he lost an eye, part of his brain, most of his hearing and sense of smell, and his face is disfigured.

Patti helps the veterans find jobs, medical support, loans, and anything else they or their families might need. Yet despite her hard work, Patti is unable to save all of them. Some get better, and some can't—Adam is, unfortunately, in the latter category.

The wife of one of her charges relates a sad story. The woman's husband was suffering from acute PTSD, but when their pleas for help fell on deaf ears, she made up a story that he was molesting their children, and he pled guilty. Now the husband is getting counseling as part of a plea deal, is on medication, and is reunited with the family.

Adam, whose marriage is rough, who is lonely and depressed and broke and misses the camaraderie of being a soldier, and who feels guilty about his struggles, consults Patti about working in private security in Africa. Patti does not think this wise and starts looking into inpatient programs for him.

Need to Know: Although the story of the veteran's wife seems shocking, she was desperate to get help for her husband. The fact that she was forced to take such drastic measures shows there is something seriously wrong with the way America handles its veterans.

When speaking with Patti, Adam mentions that he and Saskia got along better when he was going on regular deployments; he doesn't see that his PTSD is a major factor in their strained relationship.

9

On his first day in the WTB, Tausolo Aieti has gone to see former sergeant Tim Jung as part of his admission. Tim informs Tausolo that he's been certified high-risk, meaning Tausolo cannot drink alcohol, be around guns or knives, will only have a week's worth of medication at a time, and must report to his squad leader morning and night.

As part of his orientation process, Tausolo runs around the WTB obtaining signatures from various staff, including a pharmacist. Tausolo takes many medications for depression, anxiety, insomnia, knee pain, and attention deficit and memory loss. He

SUMMARY AND ANALYSIS

bumps into Sergeant Michael Lewis, who comments on his haul of pills and tells him to take the rest of the day off. Lewis himself witnessed the suicide of Jessie Robinson, a high-risk case who overdosed on pills.

Need to Know: The intense bureaucracy of registering at the WTB seems counterproductive given the mental state of many soldiers there. Tausolo's case highlights the ridiculousness of asking someone who has been diagnosed with memory problems to obtain 39 different signatures.

Tim Jung and Michael Lewis are examples of how helping other soldiers work through trauma takes its toll on their supporters. In Jung's case, the accumulation of his own pain and that of others led him to nearly attempt suicide; in Lewis's case it has made him wary of getting too close to the soldiers he is trying to help.

10

The report on Jessie Robinson's suicide is sent to Peter Chiarelli. Jessie had been home from Iraq for four and a half years. Two years in, he began exhibiting angry and abusive behavior, and in his third year back he began threatening suicide. Chiarelli is asked for a quote for a press release regarding the large number of army suicides that occurred in the month of Jessie's death, but his initial suggestion is seen as too honest about why soldiers might kill themselves, and his team revises it into a less "alarmist" version. Chiarelli and his team sit through a briefing on Jessie's death in order to see what lessons can be learned.

Kristy Robinson's own report of her time with her husband details unprovoked outbursts of aggression, violence, threats, and paranoid behavior, culminating in his suicide. When he was finally arrested for domestic battery, Kristy left with their daughter and Jessie returned to the military hospital in Topeka. Three months later, Jessie overdosed and died.

Kristy enrolls in community college, redecorates the house and starts dating Kent Russell. She sees a counselor, where she processes the anger she feels over Jessie's abusive and aggressive treatment. She admits that she felt a sense of relief at his death, but also concludes that before his destructive experience in Iraq, her husband was "a wonderful man."

Need to Know: The process of examining why a soldier commits suicide is described by a battalion commander as an "ass-pain," because any mistakes on the part of the unit will be seen as blameworthy. This makes the briefing seem more like a box-ticking exercise and less like there is genuine interest in getting to the bottom of soldier suicides.

Jessie had undergone suicide awareness training and had a card detailing how to recognize suicidal

SUMMARY AND ANALYSIS

behavior in his wallet at the time of his death. Unfortunately, given his diagnosis of psychosis and dementia, plus his paranoid delusions, it seems unlikely that Jessie would have been in a rational enough state of mind to recognize the signs and seek the help he needed.

11

Adam Schumann arrives in Sacramento to start an inpatient program, Pathway, which Patti Walker has arranged for him. After a week, Saskia is struggling and regularly fighting with Adam over phone and by text. She is alone with the kids, and is worried that she will be unable to support the family without his salary. She gets a job as a case manager at a mental health agency and is surprised by how well she takes to the work, finding she has empathy for her clients that she has lacked for her husband. One of them is a woman who ended up in a psychiatric hospital after her ex-soldier husband became severely abusive.

The relationship between Adam and Saskia continues to be tense as she becomes angry over his failure to call her until the afternoon of Mother's Day. Saskia feels frustrated and alone, Adam fails to contact her regularly, and when he does reach out, he only tells her about the recreational activities, failing to mention the hours of therapy. Soon after, she quits her job, concluding that she is not yet emotionally strong enough to help others.

Need to Know: Unlike the Topeka program, which is funded by the VA, and Pueblo, which is funded by insurance payments, Pathway is funded entirely by private donations. This helps take the weight off an already-stretched VA, which suffered cutbacks under the Bush administration.

12

Theresa Aieti calls 9-1-1 after Tausolo hits her repeatedly. The police arrest Tausolo and he spends three nights in jail, where he has nightmares exacerbated by lack of access to his medication. Once released, he apologizes to Theresa and returns to the WTB.

Tausolo undergoes therapy to help with the memory problems caused by his TBI, and starts to feel like he is making progress. A memorial is held for a 21-year-old member of the WTB, an acquaintance of Tausolo's, who committed suicide. Tausolo avoids it, finding the feelings it evokes too traumatic. He signs up for a math class at Fort Riley, having excelled at math back home in Samoa. He likes his new teacher Kent Russell—Kristy Robinson's boyfriend—who is sympathetic to the needs of wounded soldiers.

SUMMARY AND ANALYSIS

Need to Know: The rate of domestic abuse among veterans is very high. As more soldiers and veterans moved into the area, the local police had to triple the size of their department, and the frequent calls of assault, domestic violence, and suicide no longer surprise them.

Tausolo's inability to handle simple operations, such as buying his wife flowers or remembering the name of a person he just met, is indicative of deeper mental and emotional issues. Unfortunately, he is one of many veterans suffering from irreversible damage and he will have to learn how to cope with the PTSD, survivor's guilt, and TBI.

13

Fred Gusman's father was a World War II veteran who returned from combat violent and abusive. Eventually, Fred's mother took her son and fled. After doing a few years in the military, Fred worked for the VA and started the first residential treatment program for traumatized soldiers. He concluded from his experience treating thousands of veterans that intensive therapy without time limits produces the best results. Just as Fred was considering retirement, the idea of Pathway, entirely donor-funded, was mentioned to him. This would give him the freedom to run a program as he saw fit.

The younger soldiers at Pathway observe the permanent older residents with curiosity. Many of them seem to do nothing but drink all day. Adam worries he will turn into one of them if he doesn't get help.

Meanwhile, Adam feels he is benefiting from his time at Pathway and is dismayed when Saskia asks him to come home and support his family. He goes home temporarily when their son has an operation. There, he and Saskia fight constantly; she is worried about money and wants Adam to get help locally. He refuses and returns to Pathway in Sacramento several days later.

Saskia's texts and phone calls become so frequent and distressing that a counselor from Pathway calls and asks her to desist, explaining that "if he comes home too soon he'll almost certainly turn suicidal." Fed up, Adam decides to leave Pathway and drive home to his traumatized wife and kids. Partway there, he turns the car around and heads back to Pathway. This is his chance to get better and he must take it.

Need to Know: Fred Gusman's father is an example of an older generation for whom PTSD went unrecognized, and who returned from war "to no help at all. There was nothing set up for them." This is the case for the older soldiers observed by Adam—veterans of World War II, Korea, Vietnam—who are so damaged that they are permanent residents at Pathway.

SUMMARY AND ANALYSIS

Fred's desire for a program with unlimited stays contrasts that of Pueblo, where the maximum stay is four weeks, and Topeka, where it is seven weeks. Instead, Pathway has a minimum stay of four months, ensuring veterans go through intense therapy and fully process their experience without feeling pressure to "get fixed" in a short amount of time.

In choosing to stay at Pathway and getting the help he needs, Adam is taking a huge step in the right direction. But being away from his family also means they suffer. War doesn't only traumatize the soldiers—it affects entire families.

14

The recovering soldiers—Tausolo Aieti, Nic DeNinno, Michael Emory, and Adam Schumann—are distressed to hear that one of their company, Danny Holmes, has killed himself. His fiancée, Shawnee Hoffman, recalls how Danny was becoming increasingly irritable, forgetful, had stopped showering, and told Shawnee to hide his knife collection. He screamed at their infant daughter and woke Shawnee up one night hovering over her with scissors.

The night of Danny's suicide, Shawnee went out to have some drinks, got pulled over for speeding, and was booked for drunk driving. When she returned home at dawn she found Danny had hanged himself with a parachute cord.

Meanwhile, in Kansas, Amanda Doster messages Saskia Schumann to ask her to pay back the money she borrowed. Saskia replies that money is tight as she is not working and Adam is in a PTSD facility. The two message back and forth discussing their struggles and depression. The next day, Saskia is in the basement when Jaxson escapes and climbs into the backyard swimming pool. Saskia calls 911 but Jaxson is still breathing and recovers consciousness.

Need to Know: At the end of the chapter Adam messages Saskia to say "All I can think of is the death I've seen, caused." Saskia tells him it wasn't his fault, that what happened was simply the cost of war but he finds this hard to believe. They both crave forgiveness. Him, for what he saw and did in war, and his inability to support his family at home. Her, for her anger and impatience with Adam's recovery, and for almost losing their son in the pool.

15

A dinner is being planned in Washington DC on the theme of suicide prevention in the military. Peter Chiarelli wants to use it to convey the depth of the problem and get as much help as possible, but after several

SUMMARY AND ANALYSIS

congressmen pull out, the dinner ends up canceled. It is never rescheduled because Chiarelli will retire from the army several months later.

At Pathway, Adam has talked through his most difficult experiences, like when his mouth filled with the blood of his wounded, fellow solider Michael Emory, as he was carrying him to safety, and the death of James Doster. He has found the responses of his fellow group members comforting, and is now ready to graduate from the program. In his speech he thanks Fred for saving his life. He and Saskia begin the 18-hour drive home. They stop in Reno to visit family, and Christopher Golembe turns up; he and Adam reminisce about their tumultuous time together in the unit and the two find closure.

Need to Know: The implications of the loss of Chiarelli are revealed when, under the military's new chief of staff, the rate of army suicides begins to rise again "until it is exceeding the number of combat deaths and averaging almost one a day." This implies that the attitude and dedication of those in charge can have a serious impact on army morale.

Adam's words on his graduation—"I'm not cured. I don't think any of us are or ever will be"—demonstrate how healing from trauma is a lifelong process, one that may never end. But importantly, he adds, "I can wake up in the morning and smile. For the first time, I'm not thinking about killing myself every day."

16

Shawnee Hoffman is struggling in the aftermath of Danny Holmes's suicide. She is taking antidepressants and wishes she had enough money to leave the apartment where her fiancé killed himself.

Michael Emory is still living alone, visited by his healthcare aide to help him with everyday tasks. He calls his daughter in Texas. He says he feels he has been given a second chance at life.

Kristy Robinson throws a third birthday party for her daughter, Summer. She is still dating Kent but misses Jessie painfully, and her house remains full of reminders of her late husband.

Nic DeNinno has spent two years in the WTB and is awaiting his final disability rating. He has made two trips to the Pueblo hospital, and he has tried to kill himself twice during this time.

Tausolo Aieti is still taking math classes. He has been told he won't be getting out of the WTB any time soon, but is feeling better because he didn't dream about Harrelson the night before; instead, he dreamed about his son.

Amanda Doster writes a letter to Sally three days before the anniversary of James's death. Doctors have

SUMMARY AND ANALYSIS

found a lump on her neck and want to do a biopsy to see if it's cancerous. She asks Sally to finish the quilts she has started making for her daughters in case Amanda won't be around to do it.

Adam and Saskia arrive home to their children. It has been nearly four years since Adam's return from the army. Of the many differences between that trip home and this one, the biggest one is that Adam's home now "seems like the most peaceful place in the world."

Need to Know: The book ends on both a sad and uplifting note. Some soldiers survived, while others succumbed to their trauma. Finding treatment is incredibly difficult and doesn't ensure complete recovery. In fact, recovery is a lifelong process, and something with which the veterans' families also have to deal.

The rate of suicides among veterans is rising, and it's crucial that the military do everything they can to provide for their soldiers. Unfortunately, more focus goes into keeping soldiers on the battlefield than taking care of them when they're home.

Cast of Characters

Tausolo Aieti: Soldier from American Samoa who was in the same unit as James Doster and Adam Schumann, admitted to the WTB due to his suspected PTSD. He suffers from memory loss and nightmares, and he becomes violent.

Theresa Aieti: Wife of Tausolo, mother of their son, originally from American Samoa.

Alex Boland: Lieutenant in charge of Adam Schumann and James Doster's platoon, friend of the Doster family.

SUMMARY AND ANALYSIS

Peter Chiarelli: Army vice chief of staff who helped bring attention to the growing problem of poor mental health and suicide risk among soldiers.

Christina*: Wife of Stephen, who exchanges stories with Saskia Schumann about the struggle to support their injured husbands.

Nic DeNinno: Soldier from the same unit as Doster and Schumann, admitted to a Colorado psychiatric facility after his behavior at the WTB became concerning.

Amanda Doster: Widow of James Doster, mother of their daughters Grace, 3, and Kathryn, 6. Amanda struggles with the loss of her husband, who died in combat.

James Doster: Soldier killed by a roadside bomb, who served alongside Adam Schumann. His death is still mourned by his family, especially his wife. He was one of Adam Schumann's closest friends.

Michael Emory: A soldier rescued by Adam Schumann after Emory was shot in the head when their unit came under fire. Schumann is haunted by this because the blood from Emory's head wound flowed into his mouth.

Christopher Golembe: Soldier in Adam Schumann's unit who was on maneuvers with James Doster when he died.

Fred Gusman: Veteran and former VA worker who founded the Pathway inpatient program for traumatized soldiers in Sacramento. Adam Schumann attends the program and claims it saved his life.

Tim Jung: Former sergeant who now works at the WTB. He had considered suicide, himself.

Michael Lewis: Former sergeant who has worked at the WTB for three years; he found WTB member Jessie Robinson after Jessie had taken an overdose.

Jessie Robinson: Former soldier who became violent and cruel after his return from Iraq. He committed suicide, leaving behind a wife and daughter.

Kristy Robinson: Estranged wife of Jessie Robinson, mother to their daughter Summer.

Kent Russell: Math teacher at Fort Riley who teaches Tausolo Aieti; also boyfriend of Kristy Robinson.

Matthew Stern: Medic who tried to save James Doster after he was hit, and still feels guilty about being unable to save him. He becomes friends with Doster's widow, Amanda.

Sally*: Friend of Amanda Doster, described as "the person Amanda leans on most of all."

Adam Schumann: Former army sergeant diagnosed with severe PTSD, leader of the unit in which James Doster, Michael Emory, and Christopher Golembe served.

Saskia Schumann: Wife of Adam, mother of their children Jaxson and Zoe. She struggles with Adam's trauma and admits to being impatient with his healing process.

Stephen*: Friend of Adam, with whom he served in his first deployment. Stephen has TBI and PTSD and cannot work as a result of his injuries.

Kevin Walker: Husband of Patti Walker. Has been in the military for 23 years. He was severely wounded in Iraq after a roadside bomb hit his vehicle.

Patti Walker: Employee at the Wounded Warrior Program, whose job is to advocate for returned soldiers suffering from mental and physical disabilities.

---

* No last name given

Direct Quotes and Analysis

"Every war has its after-war, and so it is with the wars of Iraq and Afghanistan, which have created some five hundred thousand mentally wounded American veterans.

How to grasp the true size of such a number, and all of its implications, especially in a country that paid such scant attention to the wars in the first place? One way would be to imagine the five hundred thousand in total . . . all suddenly illuminated at once. The sight would be of a country glowing from coast to coast."

While the conflicts in Iraq and Afghanistan received vast media coverage, the struggles of veterans once they return home are all but invisible. There is little comprehension of just how hard—or, for the significant numbers who take their lives, impossible—life after war can be. Adam Schumann rages against the ignorance of those who thank soldiers for their service or sport "I Support the Troops" bumper stickers, pointing out that these are usually people who cannot imagine what he has been through, who live at a comfortable distance from the horror of war. Yet as the metaphor of a glowing America implies, traumatized veterans are all around us, all the time—we just don't realize it because so many are bravely struggling on alone.

"Look at them now, fawning over the soldiers with visible injuries, the one with gunshot scars, the amputee. And here come the inevitable thoughts. Those soldiers are injured. He's not. They're wounded warriors, and he's weak, a pussy, a piece of shit."

Since so much of being in the military is about mental strength under pressure, admitting to suffering from PTSD feels like an admission of weakness. It is especially prevalent given the largely male demographic of the military, and the way extremes of macho behavior are encouraged in soldiers. The nightmares, panic attacks, and fears of PTSD run counter to the "stiff upper lip" expected of soldiers, even though they are entirely rational reactions to repeatedly witnessing death, maiming, and threats to one's own life.

"When he comes out [Adam] is holding a loaded shotgun against his forehead. . . .

"'Pull the fucking trigger,' he yells, and what surprises [Saskia] is how much she wants to do it. She wants to pull the fucking trigger and end his life and end her misery and clean the walls afterward and be done with it, all of it. The years have caught up at last."

Saskia's reaction exemplifies how looking after a traumatized veteran takes its toll. Having put up with her husband's transformed personality with no support for her own anguish, it is unsurprising that someone might have fantasies of "ending it all" somehow. A Brown University report notes: "The military has increasingly off-loaded the burden of care for service members' health onto their families and communities, and mainly onto female spouses."

"'There were times as I would render aid to soldiers, the platoon leader said, "What about the Iraqis?" I said, "Sure," as I took my time to get to them, and it was a long time. As a medic I should take care of people, but I was pissed. So I would just take my time. . . . I gave this one guy a needle decompression for the hell of it. I know it hurt. But fuck it. As far as I knew, he had helped emplace a fucking IED. Did I care? No. Do I care now? No. Was that right? Fuck it.'"

SUMMARY AND ANALYSIS

These words from an unnamed soldier during group therapy exemplify the biggest problem for soldiers: they are trained to kill, yet are also looked to for help. The demands of returning to a civilian moral code makes the soldiers feel even more alone and abnormal. They know they lack empathy, but they have been so filled with hate by war that they struggle to retrain their minds.

"The fear of a soldier's killing himself is always there for Patti, and she does what she can to keep that from happening, by telling an employer, for instance, that yes the soldier he hired gets headaches sometimes, but the reason for the headaches is that he got rattled in an explosion fighting in a war . . . and maybe, instead of only being concerned for his business, the employer could be so kind as to set up a room with some dark curtains for the soldier to rest in from time to time until the goddamn headache is better."

The common perception is that life at home after combat must be a peaceful release. However, with physical disabilities like Michael Emory's, or mental trauma like Tausolo Aieti's, life at home may be utterly unrecognizable from the idealized state dreamed of by soldiers in the desert. It can entail uncomprehending, sometimes unsympathetic, loved ones, endless confusing bureaucracy, and a public with no idea of what soldiers have been through on their behalf. Advocates such as Patti help the soldiers transition to civilian life, acting as translators between vulnerable soldiers and often less-than-sympathetic employers and financial institutions. As Helen Benedict writes, "an alarming number [of Iraq veterans] run into employers who either have no respect for their experience or regard them as too risky to hire."

"There are two children at home as well, a young son who at one point seemed so confused by the sight of a fake eye that his father decided to stop wearing it, and a teenage daughter who one day announced that she wanted to dye her hair blue. 'We're not trash,' Patti said. 'Why?' 'So when we go to Walmart, people will stare at me instead of Daddy,' the daughter said."

The poignant words of Patti and Kevin Walker's daughter shows how army life has repercussions long after soldiers are discharged. Not only do the wounded have to adjust to civilian life, but if their injuries are obvious, as in Kevin Walker's case, they have to adjust to how they will be perceived by society at large—as disabled, even deformed. Prejudice against disabled people can range from stares and whispers to verbal and physical abuse, as well as institutional discrimination, and disabled people are more likely to suffer hate crimes. A report titled "Hate Crimes Against

SUMMARY AND ANALYSIS

Individuals with Disabilities" says, "These perceived differences evoke a range of emotions in others, from misunderstanding and apprehension to feelings of superiority and hatred."

"Money wasn't really an issue because of life insurance policies and the army's tax-free payment of $100,00, which it calls a 'death gratuity.'
    "'Blood money,' she calls it on her bad days.
    "'Oops money,' she calls it on her better days.
    "Whatever it's called, it is allowing her to make this giant leap to a new life in a new house that is 2.8 miles away."

Unlike the Schumanns, who continue to struggle with money, Amanda Doster has been able to afford a new, more expensive house thanks to the payout she received from her husband's death. The intense guilt she feels about this money is clear in her ambivalent attitude towards it. While no amount of money can compensate for such a loss, nor would anyone in their right mind rather have financial security over their spouse's life, the lack of worry about money for herself and her children is a privilege that other military families do not enjoy.

Trivia

1. In 2009, it was estimated that 20% of Iraq War veterans were suffering from PTSD, compared to 11% of Afghanistan veterans and 10% of Gulf War (Desert Storm) veterans.

2. The higher rate of trauma among Iraq veterans has been attributed to the fact that soldiers saw killing close up and witnessed their fellow soldiers dead or wounded with unprecedented regularity, and also faced "the terrifying unpredictability of guerilla warfare, where you cannot tell who or where the enemy is."

SUMMARY AND ANALYSIS

3. Army vice chief of staff Peter Chiarelli determined that the following factors made veterans more likely to take their own lives: repeated deployments with less time at home in between; being unmarried; not talking about their traumatic experiences; and having access to guns and liquor. Additionally, those who enter the army in their late twenties are three times more likely to kill themselves than those who enter in their early twenties or teens.

4. Despite the efforts of Chiarelli and his team, there is no perfect method of suicide prevention in the army: "Years of suicide prevention research and program implementation have not yet led to a definitive, highly effective, evidence-based approach to suicide prevention . . . [Furthermore] some suicide prevention training programs that have initially been reported as successful have not seen their effects last over time."

5. Applying for disability benefits is a convoluted and trying process for veterans: it involves 22 documents to be processed by 16 different information systems, "a procedure so complicated it defeats many uninjured veterans, let alone those disoriented by PTSD or TBI."

6. The Warrior Transition Battalion (WTU, later WTB) was created in 2007 and received $1 billion of initial funding. Thirty-two units were built across the country and staffed with medics, social workers, and sergeants all dedicated to rehabilitating mentally and physically wounded soldiers.

7. A 2008 study by the Heritage Group states that voluntary military recruits are more likely to be well-educated, have above-average income, and make an active choice to join the army.

8. A 2010 report found that rates of child abuse in army families were three times higher in homes from which a parent had been deployed.

9. There are roughly 8,000 soldiers in the Army Wounded Warrior Program (for which Patti Walker works), all of whom have suffered severe psychological problems after war.

10. An average of twenty veterans die of suicide per day.

What's That Word?

Department of Veterans Affairs (VA): Branch of the US government that provides healthcare, benefits, housing, and burial services to army veterans and their families.

Fort Riley: US Army base in north Kansas, from which all the soldiers in the book were deployed.

Forward operating base (FOB): A secure area away from the main base, which soldiers use to launch tactical operations. Although FOBs are defined as not having the full support facilities of a main base, they have evolved to include many creature comforts for soldiers, such as gyms and Internet access.

SUMMARY AND ANALYSIS

Gardner Room: Part of US Army senior leadership HQ, based in the Pentagon. All reports on army suicides are discussed in a conference in this room.

Geary Estates: Apartment complex in Kansas designated for military families. Tausolo and Theresa Aieti live here.

High value target (HVT): A person or resource required by the enemy to complete a mission.

Humvee: Four-wheel-drive truck commonly used in military maneuvers.

Kerlix: The brand of bandages Matthew Stern used when trying to save James Doster.

Post exchange (PX): Retail store on a military base selling goods to soldiers and their families.

Post-traumatic stress disorder (PTSD): Also called shellshock, battle fatigue, or combat stress, an anxiety disorder most common in army veterans and victims of violent attacks. Symptoms include nightmares, flashbacks, tremors, memory loss, and insomnia.

Pueblo: Military hospital in Pueblo, Colorado, dedicated to the treatment of mentally traumatized soldiers from Iraq and Afghanistan only. Not part of the VA system.

Topeka: Military hospital in Topeka, Kansas, dedicated to the treatment of mentally traumatized soldiers from Iraq, Afghanistan, and Vietnam. Part of the VA system.

Traumatic brain injury (TBI): The result of a violent impact to the head in which the brain collides with the skull, causing psychological damage. This can manifest itself in personality changes, memory problems, depression, anxiety, and nightmares.

Warrior Transition Unit (WTU): Specialist medical unit dedicated to mental and physical rehabilitation of soldiers. Later renamed Warrior Transition Battalion (WTB).

Critical Response

- A New York Times Notable Book
- A Top Ten *Washington Post* Book of the Year
- A Top Ten *USA Today* Book of the Year
- An *Economist* Book of the Year
- A *Seattle Times* Book of the Year
- An *NPR* Book of the Year
- A *Kirkus Reviews* Book of the Year
- A National Book Critics Circle Award finalist
- A Los Angeles Times Book Prize finalist
- A Dayton Literary Peace Prize finalist
- A Helen Bernstein Book Award for Excellence in Journalism finalist

SUMMARY AND ANALYSIS

"It's a testament to Finkel's considerable journalistic skills that this is no sentimental or clichéd work. His vivid descriptions of the minutiae of everyday life provide a fly-on-the-wall observation without judgment." —*Minneapolis Star Tribune*

"Finkel's real achievement is in his portrayal of individual lives. We see the men, their spouses, and their caregivers, both civilian and military. . . . Through scenes rendered with firsthand immediacy, Finkel portrays the texture of family life and friendships."
—*The Boston Globe*

"The hackneyed phrase providing the title for Finkel's fine book exquisitely captures the hypocrisy pervading that relationship [between soldiers and society]. The travails of those whose suffering he recounts give us a glimpse of the costs incurred and of who pays them." —*The Washington Post*

"Finkel is a vivid and deeply informed writer. His reporting often approaches the level of detail of great journalists like Katherine Boo and Nicholas Lemann, writers who get inside the emotional lives of their subjects without being exploitative."
—*The Globe and Mail*

THANK YOU FOR YOUR SERVICE

"This is a heartbreaking book powered by the candor with which these veterans and their families have told their stories, the intimate access they have given Mr. Finkel . . . into their daily lives, and their own eloquence in speaking about their experiences."
—*The New York Times*

About David Finkel

David Finkel was born in 1955 and graduated from the University of Florida with a degree in broadcasting in 1977. He wrote for the *St. Petersburg Times* and the *Tallahassee Democrat* before joining the *Washington Post* in 1990, where he remains a writer and editor. He established a reputation for reporting from embattled countries such as Iraq, Kosovo, and Yemen. He has also reported extensively in America, covering life on death row in Florida ,and won the 1995 Missouri Lifestyle Award for his story on race and class issues in Washington DC.

Finkel's Pulitzer Prize–nominated reporting includes features on middle-class flight from DC; a family who watches 17 hours of TV a day; a profile

SUMMARY AND ANALYSIS

of a Rush Limbaugh fan; the account of a woman's life in a Macedonian refugee camp; and the experiences of international migrants. He won the Pulitzer Prize for a three-part series reporting on the US attempts to install democracy in Yemen. He also won the Robert F. Kennedy award for his piece "Invisible Journeys," which told the stories of illegal immigrants.

Finkel's first book, *The Good Soldiers*, was an account of his eight months with a US army battalion on the front lines in Baghdad from 2007–2008. It received massive critical acclaim upon publication in 2009, and was named book of the year by the *New York Times*, *Chicago Tribune*, the *Boston Globe*, and *Slate*. It also won the 2010 Helen Bernstein Book Award for Excellence in Journalism.

Finkel said that he had received hundreds of emails from soldiers saying that *The Good Soldiers* gave them a method of conveying their war experience where previously they felt unable to talk about it. He also credits his first book with helping him earn the trust of soldiers who then allowed him access to their lives for *Thank You for Your Service*.

In 2012, Finkel was named one of 23 MacArthur Fellows and given a $500,000 Genius Award for his immersive journalism. The committee praised Finkel's "finely honed methods of immersion reporting and empathy for often-overlooked lives yield stories that transform readers' understanding of the difficult subjects he depicts."

Finkel lives in Silver Spring, Maryland, with his wife and two daughters.

For Your Information

Online

"A Legacy of Pain and Pride." WashingtonPost.com
"Ground War: The Iraq Surge the Grunts Knew." NYTimes.com
"The Iraq War in Figures." BBC.com
"The Psychological Impact of the Iraq War." ForeignPolicy.com
"True Stories About America's Military Heroes." EarlyBirdBooks.com

Books

Casualties of War by Daniel Lang
The Good Soldiers by David Finkel
The Forever War by Dexter Filkins

SUMMARY AND ANALYSIS

Friendly Fire by C. D. B. Bryan
The Forever War by Joe Haldeman
The Good Soldiers by David Finkel
The Invisible Front: Love and Loss in an Era of Endless War by Yochi Dreazen
On Killing: The Psychological Cost of Learning to Kill in War and Society by Lt. Col. Dave Grossman
Redeployment by Phil Klay
The Things They Cannot Say by Kevin Sites
What It Is Like to Go to War by Karl Marlantes
We Were Soldiers Once . . . and Young by Lt. Gen. Harold G. Moore [Ret] and Joseph L. Galloway
The Yellow Birds by Kevin Powers

Bibliography

Allison, Eric and Simon Hattenstone."'You don't ever get over it': meet the British soldiers living with post-traumatic stress disorder." *The Guardian*, October 18, 2015. Accessed January 29, 2017. https://www.theguardian.com/society/2014/oct/18/collateral-damage-ex-soldiers-living-with-ptsd.

BBC Middle East. "Iraq War in Figures." *BBC News*, November 11, 2011. Accessed February 1, 2017. http://www.bbc.co.uk/news/world-middle-east-11107739.

Benedict, Helen. *The Lonely Soldier: The Private War of Women Serving in Iraq*. Boston: Beacon Press, 2009.

SUMMARY AND ANALYSIS

Department of Veterans Affairs. "Analysis of VA Health Care Utilization among Operation Enduring Freedom (OEF), Operation Iraqi Freedom (OIF), and Operation New Dawn (OND) Veterans." 2015. Accessed February 1, 2017. http://www.publichealth.va.gov/docs/epidemiology/healthcare-utilization-report-fy2014-qtr4.pdf.

Department of Veterans Affairs. "Cognitive Processing Therapy for PTSD." 2016. Accessed January 30, 2017. http://www.ptsd.va.gov/public/treatment/therapy-med/cognitive_processing_therapy.asp.

Eckholm, Eric. "Surge Seen in Number of Homeless Veterans." *New York Times*, November 8, 2007. Accessed January 29, 2017. http://www.nytimes.com/2007/11/08/us/08vets.html.

Ehlers, Anke, Ann Hackman, et al. "A Randomized Controlled Trial of 7-Day Intensive and Standard Weekly Cognitive Behavioral Therapy for PTSD and Emotion-Focused Supportive Therapy." *The American Journal of Psychiatry*. 2013. Accessed January 31, 2017. http://ajp.psychiatryonline.org/doi/full/10.1176/appi.ajp.2013.13040552.

Farhi, Paul. "Post Reporter David Finkel among 23 Awarded McArthur Grants." *The Washington Post*. October 1, 2012. Accessed February 2, 2017. https://www.washingtonpost.com/lifestyle/style/post-reporter-david-finkel-among-23-awarded-macarthur-grants/2012/10/01/975842b2-0be5-11e2-bb5e-492c0d30bff6_story.html?utm_term=.ead64274502e.

Finkel, David. "David Finkel Talks Immersive Journalism." *University of Florida College of Journalism and Communications.* October 24, 2013. Accessed February 2, 2017. https://www.jou.ufl.edu/2013/10/29/david-finkel-talks-about-immersion-journalism/.

Hautzinger, Sarah, Alison Howell, Jean Scandlyn, and Zoe Wool. "Cost of War: US Veterans and Military Families." *Watson Institute of International and Public Affairs, Brown University.* 2015. Accessed January 30, 2017. http://watson.brown.edu/costsofwar/costs/human/veterans.

Howell, Allison and Zoe Wool. "The War Comes Home: The Toll of War and the Shifting Burden of Care." *Watson Institute of International and Public Affairs, Brown University.* 2011. Accessed January 30, 2017. http://watson.brown.edu/costsofwar/files/cow/imce/papers/2011/The%20War%20Comes%20Home%20The%20Toll%20of%20War%20and%20the%20Shifting%20Burden%20of%20Care%20.pdf.

Isaac, Michael, Brenda Elias, Laurence Y. Katz, Shay-Lee Belik, and Frank P.Deane. "Gatekeeper training as a preventative intervention for suicide: A systematic review." *University of Wollongong*

Research Online. 2009. Accessed January 31, 2017. http://ro.uow.edu.au/cgi/viewcontent.cgi?article=1240&context=hbspapers.

Kellehear, Allan. "On Death and Dying: Dr. Elisabeth Kübler-Ross and The Five Stages of Grief." *The Elisabeth Kübler-Ross Foundation.* 2009. Accessed February 1, 2017. http://www.ekrfoundation.org/five-stages-of-grief/.

The Leadership Conference. Date unknown. "Hate Crimes Against Individuals with Disabilities." Accessed January 29, 2017. http://www.civilrights.org/publications/hatecrimes/disabilities.html.

MacArthur Foundation. "MacArthur Fellows: Meet The Class of 2012." October 2, 2012. Accessed February 2, 2017. https://www.macfound.org/fellows/865/.

Marlowe, David H. "Psychological and Psychosocial Consequences of Combat and Deployment with Special Emphasis on the Gulf War." *RAND Corporation.* 2000. Accessed January 31, 2017.

National Institute of Health. "PTSD: A Growing Epidemic." *NIH Medline Plus.* 2009. Accessed February 2, 2017. https://medlineplus.gov/magazine/issues/winter09/articles/winter09pg10-14.html.

Sherman, Nancy. "The Moral Logic of Survivor Guilt." *Psychology Today.* 2011. Accessed February 2, 2017.

https://www.psychologytoday.com/blog/stoic-warrior/201107/the-moral-logic-survivor-guilt.

Stanton, Doug. "Their Corner of War." *The New York Times.* October 8, 2009. Accessed February 2, 2017. http://www.nytimes.com/2009/10/11/books/review/Stanton-t.html.

Watkins, Shanea and James Sherk. "Who Serves in the U.S. Military? The Demographics of Enlisted Troops and Officers." *The Heritage Foundation.* 2008. Accessed January 30, 2017. http://www.heritage.org/research/reports/2008/08/who-serves-in-the-us-military-the-demographics-of-enlisted-troops-and-officers.

Wong, Leonard and Stephen Gerras. "CU at the FOB: How the Forwarding Operating Base is Changing Life of Combat Soldiers." *Strategic Studies Institute.* 2006. Accessed January 30, 2017. http://www.strategicstudiesinstitute.army.mil/pdffiles/pub645.pdf.

Young, Ilanit Tal, Alana Iglewicz, et al. "Suicide Bereavement and Complicated Grief." *Dialogues Clin Neurosci.* 2012. Accessed February 1, 2017. https://www.ncbi.nlm.nih.gov/pmc/articles/PMC3384446/.

WORTH BOOKS
SMART SUMMARIES

So much to read, so little time?

Explore summaries of bestselling fiction and essential nonfiction books on a variety of subjects, including business, history, science, lifestyle, and much more.

Visit the store at
www.ebookstore.worthbooks.com

MORE SMART SUMMARIES
FROM WORTH BOOKS

CURRENT AFFAIRS

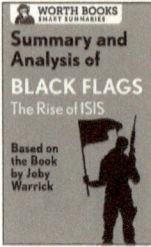

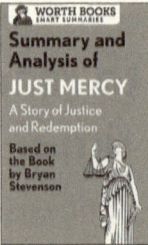
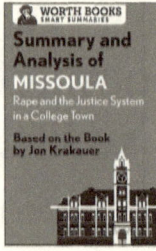

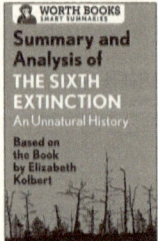

MORE SMART SUMMARIES
FROM WORTH BOOKS

HISTORY

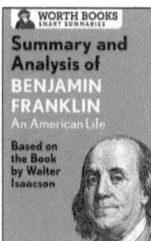
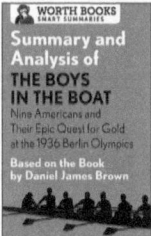
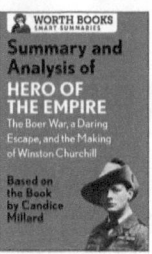
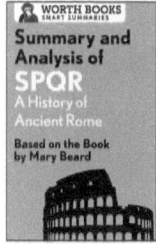
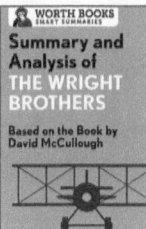
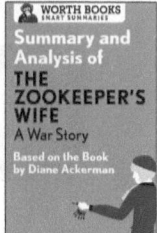

WORTH BOOKS
SMART SUMMARIES

EARLY BIRD BOOKS
FRESH EBOOK DEALS, DELIVERED DAILY

LOVE TO READ?
LOVE GREAT SALES?

GET FANTASTIC DEALS ON BESTSELLING EBOOKS DELIVERED TO YOUR INBOX EVERY DAY!

www.ingramcontent.com/pod-product-compliance
Lightning Source LLC
Chambersburg PA
CBHW022214090526
44584CB00013BA/877